The Waiters

J.A. Carter-Winward

Binary Press 2014

Published by Binary Press Publications, LLC (www.0101press.com)

Android Edition

ISBN-13: 978-1-61171-028-1

ISBN-10: 1611710286

ACT I: Little Black Facebook

SETTING

Kaiwa Japanese Restaurant--Japanese Music playing. Japanese Prop(s).

TIME

Early Evening, dinner time

Kaiwa Japanese Restaurant.

BOB

The Zen Waiter with wisdom. He is dragged into the conversation repeatedly by SPENCER and LAUREN and doles out the four truths as it applies to relationships.

LAUREN, 20

Catholic upbringing, very attached to being in a relationship with SPENCER now that they've been intimate. She has changed her FB profile to read "in a relationship". He has not. She is a student and receptionist, so she has plenty of time for social media, specifically to keep track of her 2-month old relationship with SPENCER. LAUREN is especially threatened by all of SPENCER'S female friends and followers, one in particular who is an unrequited high school flame of his.

She is never without her phone to keep up on her social media drama. She leaves it at the table for her monologues while he is busy texting/typing on his.

SPENCER, 21

Full-time student supported by his parents. He's studying fine art and is an artist (digital surrealism). He enjoys the attention of his many female sycophants who are into him and his art. In his mind, he has not been seeing LAUREN long enough to change his status on FB. Secular atheist upbringing, non-committal. He has been drinking a little too much at dinner and is slightly inebriated. LAUREN can't drink yet.

He is never without his phone. He leaves it at the table for his monologues while she is busy texting/typing on hers. They each randomly pick up their phones during dinner to text during their exchanges.

Scene 1

(LAUREN and SPENCER are already in the middle of dinner. Spencer has been downing the sake. Bob approaches their table.)

BOB

Is there anything I can get you?

(Lauren and Spencer ignore him and text. Bob looks at them both, sighs and approaches upstage)

BOB

They're busy right now. They're attached to their devices. I understand. But tonight is about intimacy, connection. Look around you. Go ahead. You see all of these people next to you? They're all here to have an experience, we are all here, together.

(Bob's phone vibrates in his pocket)

Oh shit! Okay, okay, you got me. I guess we're all attached to some degree. Ahem.

And as you can see, nothing takes you out of an experience faster than a text or phone call. Here, let's all do this together...

(He turns off his phone)

See? It's not that bad. So please, make sure your devices are off so I can better serve you. Thank you ladies and gentlemen!

(Bob exits stage. Spotlights fall fully on Lauren and Spencer.)

SPENCER

I need more sake. Where *is* he?

LAUREN

Yeah, I could use more *diet Coke.*

SPENCER

Lauren, in nine months you'll be able to drink.

LAUREN

You mean *we'll* be able to drink--together.

SPENCER

Yeah.

(Bob, the waiter, approaches)

BOB

Is there anything I can get you folks?

SPENCER

More sake!

BOB

Right away--

SPENCER

Hey what was your name again? Bob? You seem to know all about this Japanese shit--how do you say 'more sake please' in Japanese?

BOB

'Mo sake onegai shimasu.'

SPENCER

That's so cool! You lived over there, huh?

BOB

Hai. For three years. I was a student of the Buddha.

SPENCER

Oh, man, yeah I don't know hardly anything about that shit except... what is it...don't get attached or something...

LAUREN

That sounds stupid. No offense. But attachments are what make life... well, life, right?

BOB

Attachment leads to suffering. I'll get your sake.

(Bob retreats)

LAUREN

'Attachment leads to suffering.' That is so lame.

SPENCER

It's awesome. And true, I think. I mean, be free, man.

(He swigs the last of his cup of sake. Lauren crosses her arms, looking peeved.)

LAUREN

You must suffer a lot then, Spencer.

SPENCER

What do you mean? I'm completely unattached.

LAUREN

Oh really? What about me? About us?

(Lauren picks up her cell phone and begins texting. Spencer leaves his phone at the table and approaches upstage for a monologue)

SPENCER

Here we go *again*. Two months in and Lauren's talking about *us*. Hell, two weeks IN she was doing it. I get that sex is a big deal to her. I respect that. When we finally did it last week I thought she'd feel **more** secure with me, not less. I just wasn't raised to think sex was that big of a deal. But I get that it is to her. I just don't know what she wants from me. I'm only twenty-one. I'm not ready for...this.

(Spencer returns to his seat and Lauren puts her

phone down.)

SPENCER

Sure, there's you. Don't get me wrong. I like you, but he's talking about totally different shit, okay Lauren? Like possessions or something.

LAUREN

And you're attached to all of your friends. Especially your female friends. What's her name? Ashley? Yeah, you seem pretty attached to her.

SPENCER

I've known her since Jr. High, Lauren.

LAUREN

So you've said. Does she need to comment on every post you make?

SPENCER

She's an artist, too. She likes my art.

LAUREN

Every post?Even your posts that don't talk about art.

SPENCER

Facebook is about friends. Jesus. Can't we talk about something else for once?

(Spencer goes to his phone. Lauren leaves hers and stands upstage for her monologue)

LAUREN

Spencer doesn't want to talk about it because he wants all of the perks of a relationship, and all of the perks of being single. He has a thing for Ashley and it's clear she has a thing for him. Why can't she just stay in his past? I'm his present! *Me*! Right now. I-I didn't tell him he was my first. I didn't want him to know I was a virgin until I was twenty. I chose him because I love him. I haven't told him that. Just like I can't tell him I was a virgin. I don't want him to feel pressure. I feel like...I feel like if I say the wrong thing, he'll just run away. I don't want him to run away.

(She returns to her seat. Bob returns with the sake)

BOB

Here you go, sir. You like the Pearl sake? It's my favorite.

SPENCER

It's great. I like that it's cold. Hey, you have a girlfriend, Bob?

BOB

Yes...I do.

SPENCER

So does she get pissed when you talk to other girls on Facebook?

LAUREN

Spencer! I can't believe you.

BOB

I don't have Facebook.

LAUREN AND SPENCER

(simultaneously)

(SPENCER) How do you know what she's doing?
(LAUREN) How does she know what you're doing?

BOB

(laughs) Whoa, whoa...what about trust, guys? She may have a Facebook account, but I don't. I want to know what she's doing, I ask her. How was that last sushi roll?

LAUREN

You just *ask* her? Like she'll *tell* you?

BOB

Yes, she just tells me.

LAUREN

Wait, wait, you said attachment is bad, right? So how are you *attached*? (sarcastically)

BOB

I didn't say attachment was bad. Life is suffering and attachment causes suffering. But we all get attached to people. It proves the First Noble truth: life is suffering. See, attachment also brings joy. Ultimately, we lose everyone in one way or another. The price we pay for attachment is suffering. It's a part of the human condition.

(Bob leaves as Spencer and Lauren pick up their phones and text)

LAUREN

He doesn't make sense.

SPENCER

I think he's smart. I get him. He's all Zen n' shit.

LAUREN

So how attached are you to Facebook, Spencer?

SPENCER

I don't know. Not that attached. I mean it's a way to pass the time when you're bored, right?

LAUREN

I don't think you could live without it. I don't think I could. It's where you connect to everyone. Especially *Ashley*.

SPENCER

(He laughs) Connect. Whatever. It's where you post stupid shit no one cares about. And we never went out, okay? She's just a friend.

LAUREN

Right. So your art is 'stupid shit?'

SPENCER

No, ***I*** don't post stupid shit. I post stuff that matters, Lauren. Like art.

LAUREN
Oh, yeah and like your quiz results about which famous historical figure you are.

SPENCER
Leonardo da Vinci. Okay? Art.

(Lauren stands for her monologue)

LAUREN
I feel so stupid. The day after we...did it, I changed my relationship status to "In A Relationship"...he hasn't changed his. He's proudly single. So my sister tells my mother and now she suspects I did it and now... she's all in my face about meeting him and how serious we are...like I'm supposed to marry him now. And ever since last week, I feel like he's slipping away. I feel like such a bitch. I don't know how to stop nagging him. I don't know how to talk to him.

(Lauren sits back down)

SPENCER
Speaking of friends...you have plenty of guy friends on your list. You talk to them.

LAUREN
And they know about you, okay? I changed my status! Did you happen to notice that little detail?

SPENCER
Yeah. I did. I think that's something you should have, you know, talked to me about. You know? Like, people should be on the same page with that.

LAUREN
I thought we were on the same page! (Whispering loudly) W*e did it*!

SPENCER
Being in a relationship and sleeping together aren't the same things to me. Okay? I'm sorry.

LAUREN

So...so...you're, like, dating other girls? Sleeping with them?

SPENCER

Not currently--I mean, no...

LAUREN

Oh my God, I'm so stupid. I can't believe it.

(Spencer stands for his monologue)

SPENCER

I don't get how I'm the bad guy here? She didn't give me her list of expectations when she fucked me, all right? I thought that's what people did who are into each other. I didn't realize it was a fucking turning point or anything! A contract! Now I'm a big fucking jerk, is that it?

(Spencer sits down)

SPENCER

Don't say it like that, Lauren. I just don't think it's a relationship yet. We're still...feeling things out. Right?

(They both grab their phones and text. Bob returns.)

BOB

We still doing okay, folks?

LAUREN

Okay, Bob, you seem to know all the answers...what do you think constitutes a relationship?

SPENCER

Oh Jesus...

BOB

Uh...well...I think it's when two people have the same desires and needs and they share them with each other. That's what I think, anyway.

SPENCER

Ahah! The same desires and needs. See? I don't have the same as you, so we're technically not in a relationship.

LAUREN

Fine!

(She picks up her phone)

SPENCER

What are you doing?

LAUREN

Changing my status back to single! There, are you happy, Spencer? Now we're both single and NOT in a relationship!

BOB

That's a very good example of letting go. When you let go, you help relieve your suffering.

LAUREN

Well, that's great. I feel *so much better* now that I've let you go, Spencer! Free as a bird, right?

SPENCER

You didn't have to do that. (he looks at his phone) You just announced on Facebook that I'm a jerk? I can't believe you did that!

LAUREN

Just let it go, man, right? Just let it go! Don't be all attached to what I say about you. THAT causes suffering!

BOB

Not what I had in mind...I'll-I'll just go get the check.

(Bob quickly leaves)

SPENCER

Will you take it down? Seriously? How immature are you? Look, I'll put that I'm in a relationship, okay? Will that make you feel better?

LAUREN

Yes. Yes it would make me feel better. I'll take it down. (they both work on their phones)

SPENCER

There, it's officially on Facebook, okay? Does that change everything? Anything? Will you trust me now that my status has been changed? Will you stop bugging me about Ashley and my other friends? Will that put all of this bullshit to rest?

LAUREN

Sure, Spencer. I trust you now. It's all fixed. All of it.

(Lauren gathers her phone and purse and gets ready to leave.)

Goodbye.

(LAUREN leaves SPENCER there alone. BOB returns.)

BOB

Here's your check...the young lady's gone?

SPENCER

I don't know what I did wrong. I can't say what I don't feel.

BOB

But...did she even know how you feel? Do you?

(Spencer tosses his phone across the table and puts his head in his hands)

(Fade out)

(The waiter moves to the next scene/table—the

Italian restaurant--to dress for his next scene. As he gets ready, he addresses the audience.)

THE WAITER

I'm a waiter. I wait. The people I wait on wait. In the past they waited for the screech-hiss of the modem. Now, the connection is instantaneous

(Fade out. WAITER exits while GIL takes his seat at the table.)

ACT II Mis-Matched.com

SETTING

Il Forino, Italian Ristoranti-Italian Music playing.Prop(s).

TIME

Early Evening, dinner time

CAM

Server at IL FORINA. He is from a small town in Iowa. He wants to be an actor but he's terribly awkward and shy. Keeps calling MARGRET "Ma'am" which irritates and angers her. He doesn't know anything about the food or wine.

MARGRET, 56

A woman in her mid-fifties who is fighting age tooth-and-nail. She dresses young and hip. Likes adventure: dancing in clubs, hiking, skiing. First marriage was 31 years. Second marriage, 4 months to an Italian (Milanese)man 20 years her junior, with whom she is still "BFFs". Every time she says Italian words, she does it with an over-the-top authentic accent. Botox, boob job. First husband was a control freak and emotionally abusive. She set up an account on Match.com and has been dating off of that site for 2 years. She has been corresponding with GIL for a month. This is their first meeting/date. She has two grown sons and three grandchildren. She makes them call her "Maggie" and doesn't like talking about being a grandmother.

GIL, 59

Widowed after 30 years of marriage.Been single for 8 years. Started Match.com 6 months ago at the insistence of his daughter, who set up his profile. He's not even sure how it all works. Almost-retired History professor. He is deeply entrenched in his kids' lives—looking for a mother/grandmother counterpart to his family. Likes nature walks, painting landscapes and bad puns. He's dead-set on being his age—time is running short.

SCENE 1

(CAM shows MARGRET to the table. GIL is there, waiting. During their initial exchange, CAM is trying to politely interrupt)

MARGRET

Gil?

GIL

Yes, are you Margret?

MARGRET

Oh, call me Maggie...I'm so sorry I'm late! I was held up in traffic, you know how that goes.

(Margret shakes his hand and sits)

GIL

Well, yes, that's why I left early, to be here on time.

MARGRET

I *know*. I'm constantly late for *everything*. I feel like I have all the time in the world and then *poof*, it's gone!

GIL

Well at my age, you know better.

MARGRET

You're only as old as you feel, Gil.

(CAM finally gets to speak after standing there waiting)

CAM

Yes, well excuse me, I'm Cam and I'll be serving you tonight. Uh, if you want some time with the menu--

MARGRET

Yes, tell us about the wines you have tonight, Cam.

CAM

Oh, we have some really good red ones...and some white ones...

MARGRET

Okay, maybe a wine list,if you can't make a suggestion.

(Cam acts relieved he gets to leave)

CAM

Oh, yes ma'am!

(He dashes off before Margret can correct him)

MARGRET

(Calling after him) Don't call me...ma'am...and he's gone. Don't you just hate that? 'Ma'am', as if I'm some geriatric.

GIL

I always thought it was good manners, myself.

MARGRET

Well of course. You're a man. They don't have special monikers to reveal your age, do they? One day I was a 'miss', and now I'm a 'ma'am'. You've always been a 'sir'.

GIL

Yes siree.

(He laughs and she joins in half-heartedly)

I find it refreshing. Most of the waiters nowadays refer to people as 'guys'. 'Hey, what do you guys want to drink?' It's insulting.

MARGRET

We need to lighten you up, Gil. Maybe a good, red wine. We loved the *Lombardia* wines here, I wish I could remember the name...

GIL

We? So you know this place.

MARGRET

My second husband and I used to eat here *all* the time. He loved it here, said it was just like the food in Milan...

GIL

Oh, I knew you were divorced, but I didn't know...twice.

MARGRET

Well, yes, there was a second marriage, only lasted four months. It was a mistake. But *Bertrando* and I are still BFF's. We just should have stayed BFF's.

GIL

I'm sorry...'Bff's'? What does that...?

MARGRET

Oh good heavens, Gil, where have you been? It means best friends, essentially. *Bertrando* and I are 20 years apart, but it was like we were the same age, really--

GIL

He was...20 years older than you?

MARGRET

Oh, no. Younger.Such a free spirit, such an adventurer. But that was his problem, you see...he needed adventure all of the time. Especially with women, you understand. I guess I'm not as enlightened as I thought because I just couldn't share.

GIL

Well Margret, if you were married, why on earth would you share? I don't understand.

MARGRET

Oh please call me Maggie. 'Margret' is a grandmother's name. And *Bertrando*...he's, well he's just so *Milanese*. You know how the Milanese men are.

GIL

Uh, no I'm not very familiar with...the Milanese...so you don't have any grandchildren?

MARGRET

I have three, actually. And they call me Maggie, too. I just like the name Maggie.

GIL

(Gil is pleased she is a grandparent--he smiles and leans in)

Oh, so that's wonderful! Three grandchildren! Tell me about them. Boys, girls?A mix?

MARGRET

(sounding bored) Two girls, one boy. You know. They're children. I mean...they're loud and demanding...spoiled, really. But I spoil them, so I can't complain. That is when I see them which is about once a year.

GIL

Once a year? How terrible! I'm so sorry. Do they live out of state, or--?

MARGRET

Well, no. But I'm just so busy with all of my hobbies, my job at the art gallery...I mean, who has the time?

GIL

I don't know what I would do without my children and grandchildren. I mean...I *live* for them. We have Sunday dinner together every week.

MARGRET

Ugh. Don't get me wrong, I love my kids, but they're grown now. Now it's time for *me*. I gave up my youth to be a mother. Now I get to have a life.

GIL

Ehem, I...see. So, you work at an art gallery? That must be nice.

MARGRET

It's very exciting. I remember reading that you were into art--I remembered we had that in common! Let me guess...you like post-modern impressionism.

GIL

I actually, uh, paint. I like creating it more than looking at it, really.

MARGRET

Oh, so you're an ar-teest! How wonderful! Let me guess: you do...mixed media with metal, clay and newspaper! Am I close?

GIL

I, uh...well I paint in oils. I've been working on trees recently.

MARGRET

Trees.

(CAM approaches with a wine list)

CAM

Here you are ma'am--

MARGRET

You don't need to call me that. Really.

CAM

Sorry, ma'am.

MARGRET

Never mind.

(She opens the menu, points to something and hands it back to CAM)

We'll take the *Oltrepo Parvese Bonarda*, please.

CAM

That's a red one, right?

MARGRET

Yes, that's a red one.

CAM

Yes ma'am.

GIL

Sounds exotic.

MARGRET

Oh, it was one of our special wines we had, *Bertrando* and I. He was just *so Milanese,* had to have his bold reds. You know how they are.

GIL

I don't, really. No. So, uh, your profile said you loved nature. What do you like to do?

MARGRET

I love dancing naked around a bonfire in the mountains! I love to ski--I tried snowboarding last year, can you believe it? This year I want to hang glide. Or para- sail. How about you?

GIL

I love walking nature trails. It's where I get my ideas--I take photos of especially peaceful scenes, and try to paint them. I have this great walking stick my grandson made for me in Scouts--

MARGRET

You have a walking stick? Whatever for?

GIL

Well...walking.

(CAM returns with their wine. He has trouble opening it. Finally he pours. MARGRET makes a big show of smelling, swirling and tasting the wine.)

MARGERET

Mmmmm…Bellissimo!

CAM

Are you ready to order, ma'am?

MARGRET

(Looking annoyed) Yes, I'll have the *pasta fagioli* with the *insalata Italia, per favori.*

CAM

Okay, so that's number 29? And for you, sir?

GIL

Yes I'll have the number 3, the, uh, lasagna. With the salad. Do you have ranch dressing?

CAM

No, sorry sir, just the house dressing. It's--it's pretty good.

MARGRET

Ranch, Gil? Are you serious?

CAM

Ranch is my favorite, too. Back in Iowa, my mom made homemade ranch every week. I love it--

MARGRET

Oh all the way from Iowa? Well, what brings you here?

CAM

I-I want to be an actor. I just have stage fright. So I'm trying to get over that. You know. By being a waiter.

MARGRET

Oh, I see. Well good luck...with that.

(CAM leaves awkwardly)

Oh dear. So Gil, tell me. What's the craziest thing you've ever done.

GIL

Ever?

MARGRET

Ever.

GIL

My wife and I...we were at a cabin on our honeymoon and we went skinny dipping in the lake.

(GIL laughs fondly)

She was so terrified we would get caught.I was scared, too. But I couldn't admit that to her. I had to be the brave one, you know. Even though we were married, it still felt...out of bounds.

MARGRET

(she chides him with her finger rather mockingly)

Well you naughty boy. Yes. That's-that's something. Ehem.

GIL

Well what about you? Or do I want to know?

(They both laugh)

MARGRET

(She leans forward suggestively, confidentially)

I had two men at once. It was in Barcelona. *Bertrando* and I picked him up at a charming little tapas restaurant...it was such a wild night. I felt like a goddess.

GIL

Goddess gracious (he laughs at his pun)That is..is wild. I don't think I could ever do that.

MARGRET

What, share your woman?

GIL

Well that, yes, but...be naked in front of another man! I mean...there wasn't any touching, was there? I mean...

MARGRET

Oh, come on now. You're such a fuddy-duddy. I mean, really? What man doesn't want to explore the world of sex? Don't you just want to have a good *fuck* now and then?

GIL

(He looks around, embarrassed)

I guess I'm just old-fashioned. I like to be--to be in love.

MARGRET

Oh good *God*, what was it that Tina Turner said? 'What's love got to do with it?' It's about *il passione*! Like *Bertrando*...but you know these Milanese men--up to their eyeballs with *il passion!* He could never get enough, *Bertrando*. He was someone who could *finally* keep *up* with me!

GIL

What about romance and love? Don't those things matter?

MARGRET

There's a time and a place for that. Sure. But life is about *passion*, Gil. At least for me. It's why I left my first marriage. That, and he was a controlling ass. There was no passion, not ever. Him calling the shots, him deciding when and where, and if, God forbid, I had any needs... well, he didn't give two shits about that. What about you?

GIL

My wife and I were...I feel funny talking about our life in the bedroom. I'm sorry. It was private and...well, sacred to me. We had love and connection and...comfort. She was my best friend.

MARGRET

How long have you been single, Gil?

GIL

My wife passed eight years ago. She had cancer. It was very hard, but I think I'm ready to...well obviously I must be ready, I'm here aren't I?

MARGRET

You are here, Gil! You have to *move on*! Get with the program! You know there are so many singles groups to join: book groups, poetry, hiking, dining, theater--there's no reason you shouldn't be out there painting the town red! Your kids need to grow up sometime, you know. You need your *own* life, Gil.

GIL

We're a very close family. Their mother was always so good at that. She...you know, made the Sunday meals. Now my daughter and two daughters-in-law take turns...

MARGRET

But what about you! Who is Gil? What does he *want*? What does he *need*?

(CAM brings their food)

I'm not the kind of person to just sit around and wait for things to happen to me. I go out there and I grab life by the balls! I'm happier than I've ever been! I mean, who are *you* really?

GIL

Who am I? I'm just a History teacher. I like books and swing music and...I like, no, love my family. What do I want? I guess I want...I *need* order. I like routine. It makes me feel good--comfortable. I-I don't know about all of this--this social stuff. I don't know how to DO this! I don't know what I'm *doing* here!

(GIL is suddenly very upset. He stares hard at MARGRET and she stares back. They keep looking at each other as the scene fades out.)

(The waiter moves to the next scene/table—the Indian restaurant--to dress for his next scene. As he gets ready, he addresses the audience.)

THE WAITER

Perhaps I'm the devil. I present you with a menu of delights and all you need do is choose. What makes us salivate? What makes us yearn? I can sate your appetite with a wave of my pen. Or perhaps, I'm like God. A benevolent God who actually brings you everything you ask for. Or, I can deny you--"I'm sorry, but we're out of that tonight." But whether I am God or the devil, one thing remains true: we often want what's not on the menu. We sit together and order what our appetites crave, but all of our other desires, our real desires, sit between us; unspoken, unacknowledged and unfulfilled. And so we wait.

ACT III Hot Talk

SETTING

House of Bombay Indian Cuisine.Sitar Music.Eastern Props.

TIME

Early Evening, dinner time

TONY

Server at HOUSE OF BOMBAY from back east, Brooklyn or the Bronx, heavy accent. He can't pronounce any of the dishes. He pronounces *Na'an* ("nahn") *nan* (as in "tan"); *Lassi* ("lah-see") as *lacy*, and *Curry* as *cure-ee*. He pronounces *Namaste* as *na-mas-tee*. He has a talent for interrupting at odd moments.

DANIELLE, 30

Patron and wife of BRAD PARLER.

She is a yoga instructor and doing her Master's Thesis on Yoga and Mental Health.

This is DANIELLE'S first night out with her husband after discovering that BRAD has had, for quite a few years, an extensive social network of women, including dating/adult site profiles where he has engaged in cyber-flirting, cyber-relationships and cyber-sex. His screen name is Code_Man.

DANIELLE wears a cardigan on her shoulders that should be

easily removable for her monologues (she will leave her sweater on the chair back to indicate she is still at the table.)

BRAD, 31

Patron and husband of DANIELLE PARLER.

He is an CWNA (Certified Wireless Network Administrator) at the local community college.

BRAD discovered six months ago that DANIELLE had had a year-long affair with his best friend since High School, Gordon, who is also a yoga instructor at DANIELLE'S studio. Although she says she has terminated the affair, she and Gordon still work together and remain friends.

BRAD wears a hat that he will remove for his monologues (to place on the chair back to indicate he is still at the table.)

ACT III, SCENE 1

(TONY shows DANIELLE and BRAD to their table. They are clearly not at ease.)

DANIELLE

It's nice we're going out.

BRAD

Finally.

DANIELLE

What?

BRAD

You mean 'finally.' You mean *it's nice we're finally going out.*

DANIELLE

I didn't say *finally*.

(Beat)

(TONY the server approaches with water/glasses)

TONY

Okay folks, how we doin'? Welcome to the House of Bombay. *Namastee*. I'm Tony and I'll be takin' good care a ya. Now, we got some specials, some red cure-ries, some green cure-ries--

DANIELLE

I think we're ready. I'd like to start out with a *mango lassi*, please.

TONY

A lacy *mangooo*...

(he winks at DANIELLE and smiles)

And for you sir?

BRAD

Yeah, I'll just have a mango juice.

TONY

No lace for the gentleman...

DANIELLE

Also, could we get an order of *na'an* as an appetizer, please?

BRAD

Make that garlic *na'an*--

DANIELLE

I don't *want* garlic *na'an*.

BRAD

Oh that's right. Wouldn't want all that garlic to seep out of your pores during class, huh?
(Freeze motion while DANIELLE stands, pulls off her sweater to place on the chair and approaches upstage for Monologue)

DANIELLE

I cannot believe he can't let it go. I barely--no, I hardly *ever* see Gordon unless I go to one of his evening classes. It has been six months. And I have to pay the price forever?
(DANIELLE returns to her seat and places her cardigan back on her shoulders.)

DANIELLE

Well it could be offensive to people. You're lucky computers don't get offended by smell.
(Freeze motion as BRAD stands, places his hat on the chair back and approaches upstage for Monologue)

BRAD

Oh, here we go. Now it comes out. I see how she's going to play this.

(mimicking her voice)

'Those women on the computer wouldn't like you if they could see you or hear you or smell you!' I wonder what she would say if I told her that my webcam works *just fine.*

(BRAD returns to his seat and replaces his hat)

BRAD

Fine.Butter *na'an* and some *parathas.*

DANIELLE

And could you please bring an extra dish of the spicy chutney?

TONY

Extra spicy for the lady...

BRAD

Funny how you like it extra spicy when you go out, but not at home.

(Beat)

(TONY retreats. BRAD takes a drink of water)

DANIELLE

(clearing her throat)

I always have to order extra sauce. Why are Indian places so Goddamn stingy with their sauces?

BRAD

'You always have to order extra?' What, do you go out to Indian often? Oh, I guess with all the yoga crowd. They probably eat tons of Indian so they can say "Namaste" to everyone.

DANIELLE

Yes, Brad, that's exactly what we do. We go out to Indian food all together so we can say "Namaste."

BRAD

It was an observation.

DANIELLE

And a darn fine one, too.

(Freeze motion as DANIELLE stands for a Monologue)

I told him about Gordon, you know. I *told* him. I didn't have to. But I had this--this, I don't know, attack of conscience. I mean, Gordon was the best man at our wedding, for Christ's sake. In a way I felt sorry for Brad. I felt like Gordon was being disrespectful to him. I guess that's really convoluted since I was the one sleeping with him. Gordon was the one person I could count on to help me with my Master's Thesis. He's been to India, you know? Studied yoga in an *Ashram* for six weeks. I mean, he *knew* what I was trying to accomplish. *What* I'm trying to accomplish. I can't let this continue. I've got to start up on my thesis again. It just seems like every time I try and write in it...my insides start to feel all... Bruised.

(DANIELLE returns to her seat. TONY approaches with a tray)

TONY

Your appetizers, drinks and are you kids ready to order?

DANIELLE

I'm ready. I'd like the *Chicken Vindaloo*--

TONY

More spicy for the lady--

DANIELLE

I would like it hot, yes.

TONY

Some like it hot...

BRAD

(clearly annoyed, he clears his throat)

And I'd like the *Spicy Chaat*--

(DANIELLE bursts out in loud laughter)

DANIELLE

Sorry, sorry...that's just such a great *dish* for you, Brad.

BRAD

And I'd like *mine* hot as well.

(More laughter from DANIELLE as she covers her mouth, clearly unable to control herself)

TONY

Well, sir, not to challenge you at all, but the *Spicy Chaat* is quite spicy already, *knowhatImean*?

BRAD

I would still like it spicy, *okay*? *Tony*?

TONY

Oh, hey, you bet, no problemo. No sir. Oh hey, didja know that *chaat* in Sanskrit-or some kinda Indian lingo means "to lick or eat noisily and with relish"?

(DANIELLE has gained some control back, and she's wiping at her eyes while trying to keep from another fit of laughter)

DANIELLE

Fun fact! Thank you, Tony!

(Freeze action as BRAD stands for a Monologue)

BRAD

They're *avatars*, for God's sake. She's angry about some anonymous avatars! It's not like these women I talk to use real pictures of themselves. I mean, sure, Tina and Gretchen and Chloe and...what was her name...sounded like *pussy*...Lucy! Yeah. I mean, sure I saw *them* cause of the webcam stuff. But everyone else?Completely fake. How is it that women can live in a fantasy world, 24/7, but when it comes to *male* fantasy, it's all of a sudden "cheating"? I--I never touched one of them for real.

(BRAD returns to his seat and hat)

BRAD

Our waiter is getting on my nerves.

DANIELLE

Oh, *God*, he's just friendly.

BRAD

Oh yeah, when a guy flirts with you, he's "friendly", when a woman flirts with *me*, it's flirting.

DANIELLE

You just said it's flirting

BRAD

I meant "friendly". When they're *friendly* with me, it's flirting.

DANIELLE

Freudian slip.

BRAD

No, an **a**lliterative **a**llusion.

DANIELLE

Admirable.

(BRAD and DANIELLE share an embarrassed laugh. They look at each other, then bow their heads and look away, seemingly lost in thought.)

(Freeze motion as DANIELLE stands for a monologue)

DANIELLE

I--I didn't see it coming. Gordon and I had so much in common. I felt guilty knowing I shared more common interests with my husband's best friend then with him. I wasn't looking, you know? I wasn't. I should have never brought the wine that night we were working on the *kundalini* part of my thesis. It was stupid. I must have known on some level...or maybe, *maybe* I'd about had it with Brad slamming his laptop shut every time I walked into the room! You know? I mean, how stupid does he think I am? How many women do I get to share him with every day? Who are these women? These--these*bitches* who spend their *whole day* on-line talking to some guy named Code_Man? How fucking stupid is that? "I am Code_Man! Give me a coin and I can scratch off any silver coating to reveal the *secret code*!" God! They must be desperate. Totally desperate to fall for a guy without ever seeing him or talking to him. And he just preys on them. He--he has no compunction about preying on these pathetic women who are probably just looking for Mr. Right in all the wrong places, like in Yahoo Chat rooms! And his name is Code_Man, not "WannaSeeUNaked, so they think he's decent. What a *jerk*!

(DANIELLE returns to her seat as TONY appears with their meals)

TONY

Okay we got some lickedy-*chaat* for Mr. Spicy over here, and some *Vindaloo* for the spicy lady--

DANIELLE

Spicy chaat, your specialty.

BRAD

(voice raised) Yeah, my specialty! But at least it's only spicy for *me*, okay? At least I don't involve other people, *real people*, in my food choices.

DANIELLE

(voice raised) Oh yes, my *Chicken Vindaloo* is just a *hologram*, so no one gets *hurt*, is that it? Even though a real, live person *made* it--

TONY

(piping in) Kids, kids, you're welcome to share--matter of fact I'd suggest it--

DANIELLE

Oh I shared, Tony! I *shared* and now I get punished for sharing every time I turn around!

BRAD

Oh, no, I think I'm the one who shared!

TONY

(looking confused) How's about some more *na'an* for your dishes, yeah? Be right back.

(TONY walks away quickly.)

(Freeze motion as BRAD stands for his Monologue)

BRAD

I should have seen it coming. They both do *yoga* for God's sake. I mean, have you *seen* Downward Dog? Oh...oh! I'll bet old Gordo's seen her Downward Dog. Fuck! Fuck, fuck, fuck! How could she do this to me? No--how could she do this to Gordon? Did she promise him she was leaving me? *Oh my God.* She promised him she would *leave me.* It's the only explanation. That poor bastard. No wonder he's still at the yoga studio. He's like, pining for her and she just *threw* him a *bone*--ha, funny, **bone**, and then cut it off? I can't believe she could be so heartless! I mean, I'm pissed--I'll never forgive him, but we were tight, me and Gordo. Now I can't even talk to him. But he's probably so distraught over...what if she--? No, she said she cut it off. I mean...right? I can't lose her. I can't. She's everything to me. (Pause) What if she's everything to him, too?

(BRAD returns and sits, leaning forward slightly. Scene fades out. We move to spotlight on GIL and MARGRET.)

ACT III, SCENE 2

(Outside the restaurant. GIL is standing by MARGRET, head bowed. MARGRET looks anxious to leave)

GIL

Well thank you for the dinner. It was...interesting. In-in a good way, I mean.

MARGRET

Yes, well...it was. It was nice meeting you finally. We should...do it again.

GIL

Sure. Sure that would be nice.

MARGRET

I'll call you.

(She hails a taxi and hurries off-stage)

GIL

Wait! You don't have my number!

(he sighs then says to himself)

Good night, Margret.

(Fade out on GIL and fade into BRAD and DANIELLE)

ACT III, Scene 3

BRAD

Listen. You--you can have some of my *chaat.*

(Pause)

I mean...if--if you want it. I don't want it anymore.

DANIELLE

What do you mean you don't want it anymore?

BRAD

I mean I always have it. I should try your dish. I should try the *Vindaloo.*

DANIELLE

(talking softer) It-it isn't as hot as your *chaat.*

BRAD

I don't need it so hot. I mean, who needs a hole in their stomach, right?

(They both laugh shyly)

DANIELLE

I wouldn't want you to get a hole in your stomach.

(DANIELLE places her hand over her heart)

BRAD

You remember when we thought you had an ulcer?

DANIELLE

Yeah. Kidney stone.

BRAD

I was so worried about you.

DANIELLE

You took such good care of me. When it finally passed, I still wanted you to baby me.

BRAD

(Laughing) Yeah, I remember. I still brought you coffee in bed every day.

DANIELLE

Yeah, yep. You did. For a long time you did.

BRAD

I should start doing that again.

DANIELLE

Oh please, you don't have to do that--

BRAD

--but I *want* to. I liked taking care of you.

DANIELLE

Hard when you're always at the office.

BRAD

I wish things hadn't gotten so crazy at the college.

DANIELLE

They settled down.

BRAD

I know. And I kept going in too early. I don't have to be in that early. I mean, I have plenty of time in the morning to bring you coffee.

DANIELLE

How about I bring you coffee for a change?

BRAD

(Laughing) only if you sugar and cream the hell out of it.

DANIELLE

(Laughing) I know. You do like a little coffee with your sugar and cream.

BRAD

(Leaning closer to her) We used to take care of each other--all the time. Remember?

DANIELLE

I shrunk your favorite shirts.

BRAD

Not all of them!

DANIELLE

Most of them! God, I was so...so crazy! I wanted to be the perfect wife.

BRAD

You were. You are.

(DANIELLE slowly leans in toward BRAD, eyes locked. Just then, TONY appears)

TONY

Here's your *na'an* and some more water. Hey you kids like the spice? Too much? You can tell me. Burning your nose hairs off yet? Huh? Am I right?

(Freeze motion for DANIELLE/BRAD Monologue)

DANIELLE

He waited on me hand and foot. I think I fell in love with him for the first time then. I mean, I always loved him, you know? But seeing that side of him-that nurturing side to the computer wiz...it was just breathtaking. I noticed things he did that had nothing to do with who I *thought* he was.

BRAD

I don't know why I'm not satisfied with 'comfortable'. Comfortable is good. I was comfortable, and I had to screw it up by going into that chat room. That *one night* DANI goes to bed early. Then earlier, then earlier...I resented her. It felt personal, like a rejection...and I stopped being her hero. But for me I guess that was the biggest blow of all. She saw me, *all* of me. And I was just *me*. She got better...

DANIELLE

He began to surprise me with this tenderness that just spun me in circles, all of the time! I don't know how that changed, or when.

BRAD

...started her thesis and she didn't need me to...well she wanted to do *everything* all of a sudden.

DANIELLE

I don't know when he stopped being hungry to be with me.

BRAD

No, there's no excuses.

DANIELLE

I don't remember when we stopped brushing our *teeth* together. I don't remember when I began letting him match up and put away his own socks.

BRAD

Danielle didn't deserve what I did, hell, what I still do. I'm just more careful now. I would do anything to take it back.

DANIELLE

When did I stop sending him dirty texts at work or surprising him at lunch? I don't know when I stopped seeing him.

BRAD

I want to erase the memory of her eyes, looking into mine when she caught me that night. No way to hide what I was doing. It wasn't even about DANI! It was about *me*. I want to *erase the memory of Danielle's eyes*. I want to **see me** in them again.

DANIELLE

I don't know when we disappeared.

(DANIELLE and BRAD return to the table. TONY is going over the desserts)

TONY

...and we got these fried cheese balls, I'm tellin' ya, they are *muah*!(kisses fingers), and-don't let the name fool ya--somethin' called *barfivark*...

BRAD

We're fine for right now, thanks.

TONY

Oh, well you know we got the rice pudding too, so nothing weird about that.

DANIELLE

I think just the check.

BRAD

You sure? No...uh, *barfi*?

(They all laugh)

DANIELLE

No, I'm okay.

TONY

Okay kids, here's your check, and thank you for dining with us here at the House of Bombay.

(Fade Out. Lights on to the outside of the Japanese Restaurant with SPENCER. He is alone, talking on the phone.)

ACT III, Scene 4

SPENCER

Lauren it's me. Will you pick up? Look, I'm sorry. I didn't know what to say. I still don't. Will you—will you please unblock me from your Facebook? Maybe I can't say what I'm feeling, but…it doesn't mean I'm not feeling it. Call m--

(We hear a loud beep signaling he's run out of time. Fade out. Fade into DANIELLE and BRAD outside of the restaurant.)

ACT III, SCENE 5

(Outside The House of Bombay on the sidewalk. DANIELLE pulls her sweater around her and BRAD has his hands shoved deep into his pockets. They stand awkwardly side by side.)

DANIELLE

Dinner was good.

BRAD

Yeah, yeah it was...it was all right. Good food.

DANIELLE

So, you have some laundry needs or something? (laughs)

BRAD

No, no I think I'm good on laundry. Yeah, I, uh...I'm fine.

DANIELLE

You have some plans or something? Movie you wanna catch?

BRAD

(Shrugs) Nothing in the theaters I really wanna see...I mean--

DANIELLE

Oh.

(Pause)

Okay, then...

(Beat)

BRAD

I do have a lot of work coming up--you know, before the semester starts--

DANIELLE

Oh, work, huh?

BRAD

--yeah, and I could work on it at home. I mean, while you're there.

DANIELLE

Well, you'd just be working in the den, right?

BRAD

Well...yeah, but I'd be there, though, you know...I mean--

DANIELLE

No, it's fine. Maybe I can hit an evening yoga class. Then I could stop by the library after for materials.

BRAD

Your thesis?

DANIELLE

Yeah, thought I might give that a go again, you know?

BRAD

Yeah, yeah, sure...cool. Well, in that case, I'll just head to the office. Less distractions there, I guess.

DANIELLE

Oh, okay. Well...(she pauses, watching his face as he shuffles his feet) evening classes start soon, so I suppose we'll catch you tonight when you get home, huh?

BRAD

Yeah, I might be late so don't worry about, you know, waiting up for me or anything.

(They both shrug and smile at one another. Seemingly reluctant, they turn and walk away from each other in opposite directions. DANIELLE stops and turns.)

DANIELLE

(Beat)

Actually...I--I think I will wait up.

(BRAD is off stage and he may or may not have heard her.)

Brad?

(Fade Out)

ACT IV: THE WAITER

(Lights are all on one table and one chair remains. Props have been removed. THE WAITER brings out a candle, sets it on the table and lights it. He stands, addressing the audience.**Rather than have him standing there just talking to the audience, perhaps as he speaks, he slowly disassembles the set table—takes off silverware, plates, dishes, glasses and puts them on a tray behind him. Action is always better than stagnation. My thoughts).

THE WAITER

We forget that true connection requires... waiting. Yet no one connects. The one thing I cannot do is connect them.

Instead, we live in a world that makes our faces constantly turn down, instead of toward the sun and each other. We can keep past flames lit and burning when the ashes should have long ago turned cold. It's easier to look into each other's News Feed than into each other's eyes.

But when the phone is finally off, the computer silenced, the lights dimmed and the hum of solitude is upon us, all we hear is an echo of the invisible tethers that hold us together. *We are terrified of the silence.*

A man puttering around a lonely house suddenly has the opportunity for a night out with a pretty woman--mis-matched though they may be--he gets to see what's out there besides a vast sea of unknowable faces. But then words of truth are suddenly ripe and ready to be misunderstood, until they become a clash of personalities face to face.

It's a world in which a few keystrokes can result in a conversation to escape the solitude. Where we choose to take that conversation is, well, up to us. Yet, it is also a world where the penetration of words can hurt as if actual flesh has been penetrated. The betrayal justified as the glow of the LED lights wash our hands of culpability.

Our emoticons, "Likes" and cyber "pokes" wash over us, the waves in an utterly silent ocean of our own making. We wait to be returned to dry ground, with the sky above us and the earth solidly at our feet. I have hope that one day as I wait, I'll see two faces looking into one another's, as two hearts beat in real time, together. I think it's possible, if we can just take the time to connect. Until then, I wait.

(The waiter starts wiping the table Cut spotlights and then have waiter blow out the candle.)

END

Character/Setting Props

Waiter: White shirt, black pants. Black and white aprons, rag in back pocket. Order pad, pen.

Lauren: Contemporary casual clothing, cell phone.

Spencer: Contemporary clothing, cell phone.

Gil: Sweater vest or blazer with patches, plaid shirt, slacks.

Margret: "Too young for her" contemporary clothing. Bling.

Danielle: Yoga clothing, cardigan or light jacket.

Brad: Contemporary casual clothing, baseball cap.

Setting: Tablecloth, wine glasses, water glasses, plates, wine bottle/ opener, dishes (for Indian cuisine).

Japanese, Italian and Indian props such as statues or a picture.Sitar, Japanese and Italian background music.

The Waiters

By J.A. Carter-Winward

Premier Good Company Theater,

Ogden, Utah on September 5, 2014

Original Cast and Crew

Spencer:	**Jake Barnes**
Lauren:	**Charnee Jamison**
Gil:	**Paul Naylor**
Margret:	**Margaret Zeemer**
Brad:	**Allen Smith**
Danielle:	**Karli Rose Lowry**
Waiter:	**Enrique Garibay**
Director:	**Trent Cox**
Producer:	**Alicia Washington**
GCT Manager:	**Camille Washington**
Costume Design:	**Sean Bishop**
Lighting Design:	**William Peterson**

JA Carter-Winward lives and writes in the mountains of northern Utah.

Other works by the author:

Always Listen to the Ravings of a Mad Woman (under Henneman)

Falling Back to Earth

The Rub: A Novel

Grind: A Novel

No Apologies

No Secrets

Shorts: A Collection (short stories)

For licensing of this play, please contact Megan Olsen at megan@0101press.com

www.ingramcontent.com/pod-product-compliance
Lightning Source LLC
LaVergne TN
LVHW090335210926
848480LV00004B/1422
9781611710281